50 Seoul to Soul: Korean Home Cooking Recipes

By: Kelly Johnson

Table of Contents

- Kimchi Jjigae
- Bulgogi Beef
- Bibimbap Bowl
- Japchae Noodles
- Samgyeopsal (Grilled Pork Belly)
- Tteokbokki (Spicy Rice Cakes)
- Haemul Pajeon (Seafood Pancake)
- Sundubu Jjigae (Soft Tofu Stew)
- Galbi (Korean BBQ Short Ribs)
- Dakgalbi (Spicy Chicken Stir-Fry)
- Kongnamul Guk (Soybean Sprout Soup)
- Gyeranjjim (Steamed Egg)
- Kimchi Bokkeumbap (Fried Rice)
- Gamjatang (Pork Bone Soup)
- Banchan Basics
- Mandu (Korean Dumplings)
- Ojingeo Bokkeum (Spicy Squid Stir-Fry)

- Miyeokguk (Seaweed Soup)
- Dubu Jorim (Braised Tofu)
- Gochujang Glazed Salmon
- Yangnyeom Chicken (Sweet & Spicy Fried Chicken)
- Galbitang (Short Rib Soup)
- Dakdoritang (Spicy Braised Chicken)
- Kimbap (Seaweed Rice Rolls)
- Hobakjeon (Zucchini Pancakes)
- Eomuk Bokkeum (Fish Cake Stir-Fry)
- Jumeokbap (Rice Balls)
- Sigeumchi Namul (Seasoned Spinach)
- Kimchi Grilled Cheese
- Tofu Kimchi Stir-Fry
- Soy Garlic Wings
- Spicy Cold Noodles (Bibim Naengmyeon)
- Doenjang Jjigae (Soybean Paste Stew)
- Japchae Spring Rolls
- Korean Corn Cheese
- Baechu Geotjeori (Fresh Kimchi)

- Chive Pancakes (Buchujeon)
- Korean Egg Roll (Gyeran Mari)
- Beef Seaweed Rice Balls
- Dak Kkochi (Chicken Skewers)
- Anchovy Stir-Fry (Myeolchi Bokkeum)
- Spicy Tofu Soup
- Korean-Style Ramen Hack
- Stir-Fried Glass Noodles with Veggies
- Spicy Cucumber Salad (Oi Muchim)
- Braised Potatoes (Gamja Jorim)
- Sweet Rice Punch (Sikhye)
- Korean Hotteok (Sweet Pancakes)
- Yakgwa (Honey Cookies)
- Korean Iced Plum Tea (Maesil-cha)

Kimchi Jjigae (Kimchi Stew)
 Ingredients

- 1 cup aged kimchi (chopped)
- 1/2 lb pork belly or shoulder (sliced)
- 1/2 onion (sliced)
- 2 green onions (chopped)
- 1 tsp gochugaru (Korean chili flakes)
- 1 tbsp gochujang (Korean chili paste)
- 2 cups anchovy or chicken broth
- 1 block tofu (cubed)
- 1 tsp sesame oil

Instructions

1. Sauté pork until browned. Add kimchi, onion, gochugaru, and gochujang.
2. Stir and cook for 5 minutes. Add broth.
3. Simmer 15–20 minutes. Add tofu, cook 5 more minutes.
4. Drizzle with sesame oil and garnish with green onions.

Bulgogi Beef
Ingredients

- 1 lb ribeye (thinly sliced)
- 1/4 cup soy sauce
- 2 tbsp sugar
- 1 tbsp sesame oil
- 3 cloves garlic (minced)
- 1 tsp ginger (grated)
- 1/2 pear (grated)
- 1/2 onion (sliced)
- 2 green onions (chopped)
- Sesame seeds for garnish

Instructions

1. Mix soy sauce, sugar, sesame oil, garlic, ginger, and pear.
2. Marinate beef with onion and green onion for at least 1 hour.
3. Grill or pan-fry until cooked and slightly caramelized.
4. Garnish with sesame seeds.

Bibimbap Bowl
Ingredients

- Cooked short-grain rice
- 1 cup assorted vegetables (spinach, carrots, bean sprouts, zucchini)
- 1/2 cup ground beef or tofu (seasoned and cooked)
- 1 egg (fried sunny-side up)
- 1 tbsp gochujang
- Sesame oil and seeds

Instructions

1. Sauté vegetables individually with a pinch of salt.
2. Assemble rice in a bowl. Arrange veggies, protein, and egg on top.
3. Add gochujang, sesame oil, and seeds. Mix before eating.

Japchae Noodles

Ingredients

- 6 oz sweet potato starch noodles
- 1/2 lb beef (thinly sliced)
- 1/2 carrot (julienned)
- 1/2 bell pepper (sliced)
- 1 cup spinach
- 1/2 onion (sliced)
- 2 cloves garlic (minced)
- 3 tbsp soy sauce
- 2 tbsp sesame oil
- 1 tbsp sugar
- Sesame seeds

Instructions

1. Cook noodles, rinse, and toss in a little sesame oil.
2. Stir-fry beef and vegetables separately.
3. Mix everything with soy sauce, garlic, sugar, and sesame oil.
4. Garnish with sesame seeds.

Samgyeopsal (Grilled Pork Belly)
Ingredients

- 1 lb pork belly (thick-cut slices)
- Salt and pepper
- Ssamjang (spicy dipping sauce)
- Lettuce leaves, sliced garlic, chili peppers, and rice

Instructions

1. Grill pork belly until crispy and golden.
2. Cut into bite-sized pieces.
3. Serve with lettuce wraps, ssamjang, garlic, and rice.
4. Wrap and eat in one bite.

Tteokbokki (Spicy Rice Cakes)

Ingredients

- 1 lb Korean rice cakes (tteok)
- 4 fish cakes (sliced)
- 3 cups anchovy broth
- 2 tbsp gochujang
- 1 tbsp sugar
- 1 tbsp soy sauce
- 1 tsp gochugaru
- 2 green onions (chopped)
- Boiled egg (optional)

Instructions

1. Bring broth to boil. Add gochujang, sugar, soy sauce, and gochugaru.
2. Add rice cakes and simmer until soft.
3. Add fish cakes and green onions, cook until thickened.
4. Serve with a boiled egg if desired.

Haemul Pajeon (Seafood Pancake)

Ingredients

- 1 cup flour
- 1/2 cup rice flour (optional)
- 1 egg
- 1 1/4 cups cold water
- 1/2 tsp salt
- 1/2 cup mixed seafood (shrimp, squid)
- 1/2 cup green onions (cut in 2-inch strips)
- Vegetable oil

Instructions

1. Mix flours, water, egg, and salt into batter.
2. Fold in seafood and green onions.
3. Heat oil in skillet. Pour batter and cook until golden on both sides.
4. Serve with dipping sauce (soy sauce, vinegar, sesame oil).

Sundubu Jjigae (Soft Tofu Stew)
Ingredients

- 1 tube soft tofu
- 1/4 lb ground pork or beef
- 2 garlic cloves (minced)
- 1 tsp gochugaru
- 1 tbsp soy sauce
- 1/2 onion (sliced)
- 1 egg
- 1 1/2 cups anchovy broth
- Green onions and sesame oil

Instructions

1. Sauté garlic and meat until browned. Add onion and gochugaru.
2. Add broth and tofu. Simmer 10 minutes.
3. Crack in egg and cook until just set.
4. Finish with sesame oil and green onion.

Galbi (Korean BBQ Short Ribs)

Ingredients

- 1 lb beef short ribs (LA cut)
- 1/4 cup soy sauce
- 2 tbsp sugar
- 1 tbsp sesame oil
- 2 garlic cloves (minced)
- 1/2 Asian pear (grated)
- 1/2 onion (grated)
- Black pepper
- Sesame seeds

Instructions

1. Mix marinade. Soak ribs in it for 4–8 hours.
2. Grill or broil until charred and cooked through.
3. Garnish with sesame seeds.

Dakgalbi (Spicy Chicken Stir-Fry)

Ingredients

- 1 lb boneless chicken thigh (cut into chunks)
- 1 sweet potato (sliced)
- 1/2 cabbage (chopped)
- 1/2 onion (sliced)
- 2 tbsp gochujang
- 1 tbsp soy sauce
- 1 tbsp sugar
- 1 tbsp sesame oil
- 2 garlic cloves (minced)
- Rice cakes (optional)

Instructions

1. Mix sauce and marinate chicken for 30 minutes.
2. Stir-fry chicken, then add veggies and sweet potato.
3. Cook until everything is tender and well-coated.
4. Serve with rice or cheese on top.

Kongnamul Guk (Soybean Sprout Soup)

Ingredients

- 1 bag soybean sprouts (cleaned)
- 5 cups anchovy or kelp broth
- 3 garlic cloves (minced)
- 1 green onion (chopped)
- Salt to taste
- Sesame oil

Instructions

1. Bring broth to a boil, add garlic and soybean sprouts.
2. Boil uncovered for 5–7 minutes until sprouts are tender.
3. Add salt to taste and garnish with green onion and a drizzle of sesame oil.

Gyeranjjim (Steamed Egg)

Ingredients

- 3 eggs
- 1/2 cup water or anchovy broth
- 1/4 tsp salt
- 1/2 green onion (chopped)
- Sesame oil (optional)

Instructions

1. Whisk eggs, water, and salt until smooth.
2. Strain mixture into a heatproof bowl.
3. Steam on low heat for 10–12 minutes until just set.
4. Garnish with green onion and a drop of sesame oil.

Kimchi Bokkeumbap (Fried Rice)

Ingredients

- 1 cup kimchi (chopped)
- 2 cups cold rice
- 1/2 onion (diced)
- 1 tbsp gochujang
- 1 tbsp soy sauce
- 1 egg (optional)
- Sesame oil and seeds

Instructions

1. Sauté onion and kimchi until caramelized.
2. Add rice, gochujang, and soy sauce. Stir-fry until evenly mixed.
3. Top with a fried egg and garnish with sesame oil and seeds.

Gamjatang (Pork Bone Soup)

Ingredients

- 1.5 lbs pork neck bones
- 2 potatoes (chopped)
- 1/4 Napa cabbage (sliced)
- 1 tbsp doenjang (soybean paste)
- 2 tbsp gochugaru
- 1 tbsp perilla seed powder (optional)
- 3 cloves garlic (minced)
- 1 green onion (chopped)

Instructions

1. Parboil bones for 5 minutes. Drain and rinse.
2. Simmer in fresh water with doenjang and garlic for 30 minutes.
3. Add potatoes, cabbage, and gochugaru. Simmer another 30 minutes.
4. Add perilla seed powder and green onion before serving.

Banchan Basics
Includes:

- **Kimchi** – fermented napa cabbage with gochugaru and garlic

- **Sigeumchi Namul** – blanched spinach with sesame oil and garlic

- **Oi Muchim** – spicy cucumber salad with vinegar and gochugaru

- **Gaji Namul** – steamed eggplant dressed in soy sauce, sesame oil, and garlic

- **Gyeran Mari** – rolled omelet with scallions and carrots

Mandu (Korean Dumplings)

Ingredients

- 1/2 lb ground pork or beef
- 1 cup Napa cabbage (chopped, salted, and squeezed)
- 1/4 cup tofu (crumbled)
- 1/4 cup green onion (chopped)
- 1 tsp garlic (minced)
- Salt and pepper
- Mandu wrappers

Instructions

1. Mix filling ingredients. Spoon into wrappers and seal.
2. Pan-fry until golden or steam for a softer texture.
3. Serve with dipping sauce (soy sauce, vinegar, sesame oil).

Ojingeo Bokkeum (Spicy Squid Stir-Fry)

Ingredients

- 1 squid (cleaned and sliced)
- 1/2 onion (sliced)
- 1/2 carrot (julienned)
- 1/2 bell pepper (sliced)
- 1 tbsp gochujang
- 1 tbsp soy sauce
- 1 tbsp sugar
- 2 garlic cloves (minced)
- 1 tsp sesame oil

Instructions

1. Mix sauce ingredients in a bowl.
2. Stir-fry veggies and squid over high heat.
3. Add sauce and cook until everything is coated and squid is cooked through.
4. Finish with sesame oil.

Miyeokguk (Seaweed Soup)

Ingredients

- 1/4 cup dried miyeok (seaweed), soaked and drained
- 1/4 lb beef (sliced thin)
- 1 tbsp soy sauce
- 1 clove garlic (minced)
- 5 cups water or anchovy broth
- Sesame oil

Instructions

1. Sauté beef and seaweed in sesame oil.
2. Add water and bring to a boil.
3. Simmer for 20–30 minutes.
4. Season with soy sauce and serve warm.

Dubu Jorim (Braised Tofu)

Ingredients

- 1 block firm tofu (sliced and pan-fried)
- 1 tbsp soy sauce
- 1 tsp sugar
- 1 tsp sesame oil
- 1 garlic clove (minced)
- 1 green onion (chopped)
- 1 tsp gochugaru (optional)

Instructions

1. Pan-fry tofu slices until golden on both sides.
2. Mix sauce and pour over tofu.
3. Simmer for 5–10 minutes until sauce thickens.
4. Garnish with green onion and sesame seeds.

Gochujang Glazed Salmon

Ingredients

- 2 salmon fillets
- 1 tbsp gochujang
- 1 tbsp soy sauce
- 1 tbsp honey
- 1 tsp sesame oil
- 1 garlic clove (minced)

Instructions

1. Mix glaze ingredients.
2. Brush over salmon and bake at 400°F for 12–15 minutes.
3. Broil for the last 2 minutes to caramelize glaze.
4. Serve with rice and steamed greens.

Yangnyeom Chicken (Sweet & Spicy Fried Chicken)
Ingredients

- 1 lb chicken (wings or boneless chunks)
- Salt and pepper
- 1/2 cup cornstarch
- Oil for frying

Sauce

- 2 tbsp gochujang
- 1 tbsp ketchup
- 1 tbsp honey
- 1 tbsp soy sauce
- 1 tbsp minced garlic
- 1 tsp vinegar

Instructions

1. Season and coat chicken with cornstarch. Fry until golden and crispy.
2. In a pan, heat sauce until bubbling.
3. Toss fried chicken in sauce until coated.
4. Garnish with sesame seeds and green onions.

Galbitang (Short Rib Soup)

Ingredients:

- 2 lbs beef short ribs
- 12 cups water
- 1 Korean radish (mu), cut into thick slices
- 6 cloves garlic, crushed
- 1 medium onion, halved
- 4 green onions, chopped
- Salt and pepper to taste
- Optional: glass noodles (dangmyeon), soaked

Instructions:

1. Soak the short ribs in cold water for 1 hour to remove excess blood. Drain and rinse.
2. In a large pot, bring ribs and 12 cups of water to a boil. Skim off foam.
3. Add radish, garlic, and onion. Simmer for 1.5–2 hours until ribs are tender.
4. Remove radish and ribs. Slice radish and return to pot.
5. Add chopped green onions. Season with salt and pepper.
6. Optional: Add soaked glass noodles just before serving.

Dakdoritang (Spicy Braised Chicken)

Ingredients:

- 1 whole chicken, cut into pieces
- 2 potatoes, chopped
- 1 carrot, chopped
- 1 onion, sliced
- 2 cups water
- 3 tbsp gochugaru (Korean red pepper flakes)
- 2 tbsp gochujang (red chili paste)
- 2 tbsp soy sauce
- 1 tbsp sugar
- 1 tbsp minced garlic
- 1 tsp sesame oil

Instructions:

1. Combine gochugaru, gochujang, soy sauce, sugar, garlic, and sesame oil to make the sauce.
2. In a large pot, place chicken, veggies, sauce, and water.
3. Bring to a boil, then simmer for 30–40 minutes until chicken is cooked and sauce thickens.
4. Serve hot with rice.

Kimbap (Seaweed Rice Rolls)

Ingredients:

- 4 sheets gim (roasted seaweed)
- 2 cups cooked short-grain rice
- 1 tsp sesame oil
- 1/2 tsp salt
- Fillings: julienned carrot, spinach, pickled radish, egg strips, crab stick or bulgogi

Instructions:

1. Mix rice with sesame oil and salt.
2. Place seaweed shiny-side down on a bamboo mat.
3. Spread rice thinly over 3/4 of the seaweed.
4. Lay fillings horizontally across the rice.
5. Roll tightly and slice into bite-sized rounds.
6. Serve with soy sauce or as-is.

Hobakjeon (Zucchini Pancakes)

Ingredients:

- 1 zucchini, thinly sliced
- 1 egg
- 1/4 cup flour
- Salt to taste
- Oil for pan-frying

Instructions:

1. Lightly salt the zucchini slices and let sit 10 minutes.
2. Dust each slice with flour, then dip in beaten egg.
3. Pan-fry until golden on both sides.
4. Serve with a dipping sauce of soy sauce, vinegar, and sesame seeds.

Eomuk Bokkeum (Fish Cake Stir-Fry)

Ingredients:

- 1 package Korean fish cakes, sliced
- 1/2 onion, sliced
- 1/2 bell pepper, sliced
- 1 tbsp soy sauce
- 1 tsp sugar
- 1 clove garlic, minced
- 1 tsp sesame oil
- 1 tsp sesame seeds

Instructions:

1. Stir-fry onion and garlic in oil for 1 minute.
2. Add fish cakes and bell pepper, cook 2–3 minutes.
3. Add soy sauce, sugar, and sesame oil. Stir-fry another 2 minutes.
4. Garnish with sesame seeds.

Jumeokbap (Rice Balls)

Ingredients:

- 2 cups cooked rice
- 1 tsp sesame oil
- 1/4 tsp salt
- 2 tbsp furikake or crushed seaweed
- Optional: tuna, kimchi, or avocado for filling

Instructions:

1. Mix rice with sesame oil, salt, and furikake.
2. Wet hands, take a small amount of rice, and shape into balls.
3. Optional: place a small filling in the center before shaping.
4. Serve as a snack or side.

Sigeumchi Namul (Seasoned Spinach)

Ingredients:

- 1 lb fresh spinach
- 1 tsp sesame oil
- 1 tbsp soy sauce
- 1 tsp minced garlic
- 1 tsp sesame seeds
- 1/2 tsp sugar
- Pinch of salt

Instructions:

1. Boil spinach in water for 1–2 minutes until wilted.
2. Drain and rinse with cold water to stop cooking.
3. Squeeze out excess water and chop the spinach.
4. Toss the spinach with sesame oil, soy sauce, garlic, sugar, salt, and sesame seeds.
5. Serve chilled or at room temperature.

Kimchi Grilled Cheese

Ingredients:

- 2 slices sourdough or your favorite bread
- 2 tbsp butter
- 1/2 cup shredded cheddar cheese
- 1/4 cup chopped kimchi
- 1 tbsp mayonnaise (optional)

Instructions:

1. Spread butter on one side of each bread slice.
2. On the other side of one slice, spread a thin layer of mayonnaise (optional) and top with cheddar cheese.
3. Add a generous layer of chopped kimchi and top with another slice of bread, butter side out.
4. Grill on medium heat, flipping halfway, until the bread is golden and the cheese is melted.

Tofu Kimchi Stir-Fry

Ingredients:

- 1 block firm tofu, cubed
- 1/2 cup kimchi, chopped
- 1 tbsp soy sauce
- 1 tbsp sesame oil
- 1 tbsp gochujang (Korean chili paste)
- 1 tsp sugar
- 1 clove garlic, minced
- 1 tsp sesame seeds

Instructions:

1. Drain and press tofu to remove excess moisture, then cut it into cubes.
2. Heat sesame oil in a pan over medium heat and fry tofu until golden on all sides.
3. Add garlic and cook for another minute.
4. Stir in kimchi, soy sauce, gochujang, and sugar, cooking for 2-3 minutes until the kimchi is softened and everything is well-coated.
5. Garnish with sesame seeds and serve.

Soy Garlic Wings

Ingredients:

- 10 chicken wings
- 2 tbsp soy sauce
- 2 tbsp honey
- 1 tbsp sesame oil
- 3 cloves garlic, minced
- 1 tsp rice vinegar
- 1 tsp sesame seeds
- 1/2 tsp black pepper

Instructions:

1. Preheat oven to 400°F (200°C). Line a baking sheet with foil or parchment paper.
2. Mix soy sauce, honey, sesame oil, garlic, rice vinegar, and black pepper in a bowl.
3. Coat the chicken wings with the marinade and let them sit for at least 30 minutes.
4. Bake for 20–25 minutes, flipping halfway through, until crispy and golden.
5. Sprinkle with sesame seeds and serve.

Spicy Cold Noodles (Bibim Naengmyeon)

Ingredients:

- 1 package naengmyeon noodles (buckwheat noodles)
- 1 tbsp gochujang (Korean chili paste)
- 1 tbsp rice vinegar
- 1 tsp sesame oil
- 1 tbsp sugar
- 1/2 cucumber, julienned
- 1/2 boiled egg, halved
- 1 tbsp sesame seeds
- Kimchi, for garnish (optional)

Instructions:

1. Cook naengmyeon noodles according to the package instructions. Drain and rinse under cold water to cool them.
2. In a small bowl, mix gochujang, rice vinegar, sesame oil, and sugar to make the sauce.
3. Toss the cooled noodles with the sauce until evenly coated.
4. Top with cucumber, boiled egg halves, sesame seeds, and kimchi if desired.

Doenjang Jjigae (Soybean Paste Stew)

Ingredients:

- 1/4 cup doenjang (fermented soybean paste)
- 6 cups water or vegetable broth
- 1/2 onion, sliced
- 1 zucchini, sliced
- 1/2 block tofu, cubed
- 2 green chilies, sliced
- 2 cloves garlic, minced
- 1 tbsp sesame oil
- 1 tbsp gochugaru (Korean red pepper flakes)
- 1/4 cup green onions, chopped

Instructions:

1. Heat sesame oil in a large pot and sauté onions and garlic until fragrant.
2. Add water or broth and bring to a boil.
3. Stir in doenjang, gochugaru, zucchini, tofu, and green chilies. Simmer for 10–15 minutes.
4. Adjust seasoning with additional doenjang or salt if needed.
5. Garnish with green onions before serving.

Japchae Spring Rolls

Ingredients:

- 1 cup cooked japchae (Korean sweet potato noodles with veggies)
- Rice paper wrappers
- Lettuce leaves
- Optional: avocado, julienned cucumber, or grilled tofu

Instructions:

1. Dip rice paper into warm water to soften.
2. Lay on a flat surface and place a lettuce leaf, a few spoonfuls of japchae, and any additional fillings.
3. Fold the sides and roll tightly like a burrito.
4. Serve with soy dipping sauce or spicy gochujang vinaigrette.

Korean Corn Cheese

Ingredients:

- 1 can sweet corn, drained
- 1 tbsp mayonnaise
- 1 tbsp sugar
- 1 tbsp butter
- 1 cup mozzarella cheese

Instructions:

1. Heat butter in a pan and sauté corn for 2–3 minutes.
2. Stir in mayo and sugar. Cook 1 more minute.
3. Top with mozzarella and broil until cheese is bubbly and golden.
4. Serve hot in a skillet or small dish.

Baechu Geotjeori (Fresh Kimchi)

Ingredients:

- 1 small napa cabbage, chopped
- 1 tbsp salt
- 1 tbsp fish sauce
- 1 tbsp gochugaru (Korean red pepper flakes)
- 2 cloves garlic, minced
- 1/2 tsp sugar
- 2 green onions, chopped

Instructions:

1. Sprinkle salt on cabbage and let sit for 30 minutes. Rinse and drain.
2. Mix garlic, gochugaru, sugar, fish sauce, and green onions.
3. Toss cabbage in the seasoning mix.
4. Eat immediately or refrigerate for 1–2 days.

Chive Pancakes (Buchujeon)

Ingredients:

- 1 bunch garlic chives, chopped
- 1/2 cup flour
- 1/4 cup water
- 1 egg
- Salt to taste
- Oil for frying

Instructions:

1. Mix all ingredients into a thick batter.
2. Heat oil in a pan and pour batter to form thin pancakes.
3. Fry until golden on both sides.
4. Serve with soy dipping sauce.

Korean Egg Roll (Gyeran Mari)

Ingredients:

- 3 eggs
- 1 tbsp finely chopped carrot
- 1 tbsp chopped green onion
- Pinch of salt
- Oil for frying

Instructions:

1. Beat eggs with veggies and salt.
2. Pour a thin layer into an oiled non-stick pan.
3. Once set, roll gently, then push to one side. Add more egg and repeat rolling.
4. Slice into bite-size pieces.

Beef Seaweed Rice Balls

Ingredients:

- 1 cup cooked short-grain rice
- 1/2 cup cooked ground beef (seasoned with soy sauce, sugar, garlic)
- 1 tsp sesame oil
- Crushed roasted seaweed
- Optional: gochujang for dipping

Instructions:

1. Mix rice, beef, and sesame oil.
2. Shape into balls and roll in crushed seaweed.
3. Chill slightly before serving for firmer texture.

Dak Kkochi (Chicken Skewers)

Ingredients:

- 1 lb chicken thighs, cubed
- 1 tbsp soy sauce
- 1 tbsp gochujang
- 1 tbsp honey
- 1 tbsp sesame oil
- Skewers

Instructions:

1. Marinate chicken in sauce for 30 minutes.
2. Thread onto skewers and grill or pan-fry until cooked.
3. Brush with leftover marinade and garnish with sesame seeds.

Anchovy Stir-Fry (Myeolchi Bokkeum)

Ingredients:

- 1 cup dried anchovies (small size)
- 1 tsp oil
- 1 tbsp soy sauce
- 1 tsp sugar
- 1 tsp honey or corn syrup
- 1 tsp minced garlic
- Toasted sesame seeds

Instructions:

1. Dry roast anchovies until fragrant.
2. Stir-fry with oil and garlic.
3. Add soy sauce, sugar, and honey. Stir until coated.
4. Sprinkle with sesame seeds.

Spicy Tofu Soup

Ingredients:

- 1 block soft tofu, cubed
- 2 cups vegetable broth
- 1 tbsp gochugaru
- 1 tbsp soy sauce
- 1 clove garlic, minced
- 1 green onion, chopped

Instructions:

1. Bring broth to a simmer with gochugaru, soy sauce, and garlic.
2. Add tofu and gently heat through.
3. Finish with green onion and serve with rice.

Korean-Style Ramen Hack

Ingredients:

- 1 pack instant ramen
- 1 egg
- 1 slice cheese
- 1 green onion, chopped
- 1/2 tsp sesame oil
- Optional: kimchi or spam

Instructions:

1. Cook ramen with seasoning.
2. Crack in egg and simmer until just set.
3. Add cheese slice and sesame oil.
4. Top with green onions and extras like kimchi.

Stir-Fried Glass Noodles with Veggies

Ingredients:

- 4 oz sweet potato glass noodles (dangmyeon), cooked
- 1/2 onion, sliced
- 1/2 carrot, julienned
- 1/2 cup spinach, blanched
- 1/4 bell pepper, sliced
- 1 tbsp soy sauce
- 1 tsp sugar
- 1 tsp sesame oil
- 1 tsp sesame seeds

Instructions:

1. Stir-fry all veggies with a little oil.
2. Add cooked noodles and seasoning.
3. Toss until well coated and glossy.
4. Sprinkle with sesame seeds and serve.

Spicy Cucumber Salad (Oi Muchim)

Ingredients:

- 2 Persian cucumbers (or 1 English cucumber), thinly sliced
- 1/2 tsp salt
- 1 clove garlic, minced
- 1 tbsp gochugaru (Korean red pepper flakes)
- 1 tsp sugar
- 1 tbsp rice vinegar
- 1 tsp soy sauce
- 1 tsp sesame oil
- 1 tsp sesame seeds

Instructions:

1. Sprinkle sliced cucumbers with salt, mix, and let sit for 10 minutes.
2. Drain any excess moisture.
3. Toss with garlic, gochugaru, sugar, vinegar, soy sauce, and sesame oil.
4. Garnish with sesame seeds and serve chilled.

Braised Potatoes (Gamja Jorim)

Ingredients:

- 2 medium potatoes, cubed
- 1 tbsp soy sauce
- 1 tsp sugar
- 1 tbsp corn syrup or honey
- 1/2 cup water
- 1 tsp sesame oil
- 1 clove garlic, minced
- 1 tsp toasted sesame seeds

Instructions:

1. In a pan, combine potatoes, water, soy sauce, sugar, and garlic.
2. Bring to a simmer, cover, and cook until potatoes are tender (about 10–12 minutes).
3. Remove lid, stir in corn syrup or honey, and reduce the sauce until thick and glossy.
4. Finish with sesame oil and sesame seeds.

Sweet Rice Punch (Sikhye)

Ingredients:

- 1/2 cup malted barley powder (or malt water)
- 1 cup cooked short-grain rice
- 6 cups water
- 1/2 cup sugar (adjust to taste)
- Pine nuts (optional)

Instructions:

1. Mix malt powder with 2 cups warm water, let settle, and pour off the clear water (discard the sediment).
2. Add this clear liquid to a pot with 4 more cups water and cooked rice.
3. Keep the mixture warm (around 130°F/54°C) for 4–5 hours until rice grains float.
4. Strain and sweeten with sugar. Chill thoroughly before serving.
5. Garnish with pine nuts if desired.

Korean Hotteok (Sweet Pancakes)

Ingredients for dough:

- 1 cup warm milk
- 2 tbsp sugar
- 2 tsp active dry yeast
- 2 cups flour
- 1/2 tsp salt

Filling:

- 1/2 cup brown sugar
- 1/2 tsp cinnamon
- 1/4 cup chopped walnuts or peanuts

Instructions:

1. Mix warm milk, sugar, and yeast. Let it foam (5–10 min).
2. Add flour and salt. Knead into a soft dough, cover, and let rise 1 hour.
3. Divide dough into balls, flatten, and fill with the brown sugar-nut mix.
4. Pinch closed, then flatten into disks.
5. Fry on medium heat until golden and caramel inside is gooey.

Yakgwa (Honey Cookies)

Ingredients:

- 2 cups flour
- 1/2 tsp ginger juice (optional)
- 1/4 cup sesame oil
- 1/4 cup soju or white wine
- Pinch of salt

Honey Syrup:

- 1/2 cup honey
- 1/2 cup rice syrup or corn syrup
- 1/4 cup water
- 1 tbsp sugar

Instructions:

1. Mix flour, sesame oil, ginger juice, soju, and salt into a soft dough.
2. Roll out and cut into flower or diamond shapes.
3. Deep-fry on low heat until golden and crisp.
4. Simmer syrup ingredients, then soak cookies in warm syrup for 1–2 hours.
5. Drain and serve.

Korean Iced Plum Tea (Maesil-cha)

Ingredients:

- 3 tbsp maesil-cheong (Korean green plum syrup)
- 1 cup cold water or sparkling water
- Ice
- Optional: sliced plum or mint leaves

Instructions:

1. Mix maesil-cheong with cold water.
2. Stir well and pour over ice.
3. Garnish with a plum slice or mint for a refreshing twist.

www.ingramcontent.com/pod-product-compliance
Lightning Source LLC
LaVergne TN
LVHW061951070526
838199LV00060B/4077